MARIE-ANTOINETTE

The Queen and the French Revolution

Written by Benoît-J. Pédretti
Translated by Rebecca Neal

History 50MINUTES.com

MARIE-ANTOINETTE

KEY INFORMATION

- **Born:** 2 November 1755 in Vienna.
- **Died:** 16 October 1793 in Paris.
- **Role:** Queen of France from 1774 to 1791.
- **Key life events:**
  - The second-youngest child of Francis I, Holy Roman Emperor (1708-1765) and Empress Maria Theresa (1717-1780), at the age of 14 Marie-Antoinette became a crucial pawn in the late 18th-century game of diplomatic alliances in Europe. Her mother, who wanted to secure an alliance with France, promised her in marriage to the dauphin Louis-Auguste (1754-1793), the grandson of Louis XV (1710-1774) and therefore heir apparent to the French throne. The two were married on 19 April 1770, first by proxy at the Augustinian Church in Vienna, and then at Versailles on 16 May 1770.
  - When King Louis XV died on 10 May 1774, the dauphine became Queen of France and Navarre. The happy and cheerful new queen was in the middle of a brilliant society, among which were a few favourites. They lived a lavish life at the Palace of Versailles, the Petit Trianon and the Hameau de la Reine, surrounded by the schemes, gossip and intrigues of the court.
  - Throughout the French Revolution, which began in 1789, she was the focus of the discontent of the populace, and her unpopularity grew until the royal family fled to Varennes on 20 June 1791, at which point all respect for her was lost. On 10 August 1792, revolu-

tionaries stormed the Tuileries Palace and imprisoned Marie-Antoinette in the Temple, which became a prison, and then in the Conciergerie until her execution. She was guillotined in the Place de la Révolution in Paris on 16 October 1793.

○ Her premature death at the age of 37, at the height of the revolutionary upheaval, made her one of the foremost legendary figures in the history of France. At once the target of criticism and a subject of compassion, she opened up an inexhaustible and controversial debate.

INTRODUCTION

Marie-Antoinette, Archduchess of Austria, grew up at the court in Vienna with her 15 brothers and sisters. At the age of 14, she married Louis-Auguste, the grandson of King Louis XV. Marie-Antoinette was now dauphine, and the young girl was released with no precautions into the middle of the intrigues of the court at Versailles, where countless rival factions opposed one another. When she became Queen of France on 10 May 1774, as the wife of the timid and simple Louis XVI, she led a frivolous and carefree existence centred around the theatre and games, away from all political wrangling. The victim of a smear campaign in the Affair of the Diamond Necklace which shook France in 1785-1786, she did not take care to protect her public image, which was gradually becoming tarnished.

While the Estates-General were threatening the monarchy, her second son, the dauphin Louis-Joseph (1781-1789), died in June 1789 at the age of eight. Disoriented and swept away by the revolutionary upheaval, she struggled in the middle of events that she did not fully grasp. She was placed under house arrest in the Tuileries Palace in 1790, before escaping along with the rest of the royal family to go to Varennes. However, she was stopped on the way and brought back to Paris by force in June 1791, where she was imprisoned in the Temple. After the execution of Louis XVI on 21 January 1793, her children were taken away from her. On 2 August, she was finally led to the Conciergerie as a prisoner to await her trial. She was sentenced by the Revolutionary Tribunal on 16 October 1793 and guillotined on the same day.

An iconic figure of the Royalist cause and exalted by Romantic historians during the 19th century, Marie-Antoinette nonetheless remains a controversial character, sometimes dismissed as an inconsequential beauty, sometimes seen as the Machiavellian influence behind the Counter-Revolution.

THE LIFE OF MARIE-ANTOINETTE

A YOUNG ARCHDUCHESS IN VIENNA (1755-1770)

Marie-Antoinette was the 15th and second youngest child of Francis III of Lorraine, who became Francis I, Holy Roman Emperor, in 1745, and his wife Maria Theresa, Archduchess of Austria and heiress to the vast Habsburg dominions. The mischievous and absent-minded young girl divided her time between the Hofburg Palace and Schönbrunn in Vienna, with her many brothers and sisters, in an atmosphere of moderate luxury and without the strict and oppressive etiquette of the French or Spanish courts.

When Francis I died, his wife Empress Maria Theresa decided to take charge of her children's destinies. Her eldest son, the future Joseph II (1741-1790) was chosen to become emperor and took his place alongside his mother. Maria Theresa chose a far better match for Marie-Antoinette than for her other children, promising her to the heir to the French throne. The Abbé de Vermond, a doctor at the Sorbonne, was selected to teach the future dauphine about the customs of Versailles. It was essential that she spoke French, and her appearance needed to be reviewed.

By the spring of 1770, she was finally ready. Her wedding took place on 19 April at the Augustinian Church in Vienna, by proxy, as had been the case for King Louis XIV (1638-1715). A few days later, she said goodbye to her mother and left the court in Vienna, never to return. She was not yet 15, and had never met her husband.

A DAUPHINE AT VERSAILLES (1770-1774)

A procession of 57 coaches and 132 people then set off from Vienna on the 24-day journey across the Holy Roman Empire to France. The procession reached Strasbourg on 7 May 1770, then Lorraine, the homeland of Marie-Antoinette's paternal ancestors, which has recently become part of France again, and Champagne. Finally, King Louis XV came to meet her on the bridge of Berne in the forest of Compiègne. He was accompanied by his grandson, who timidly kissed her on the cheek. On 16 May, she entered Versailles, where she married the dauphin. The wedding was followed by lavish festivities: an opera by Lully (French-Italian composer, 1632-1687), an opera by Rameau (French composer, 1683-1764), and enchanting fireworks in both Versailles and Paris. The celebrations continued until the middle of July.

Marie-Antoinette's wedding celebrations in the opera hall at Versailles, 1770.

Marie-Antoinette struggled to adapt to the strict rules of the formal etiquette at court, which forbade all intimacy. Furthermore, her husband neglected her to go out hunting. She was bored and trapped between the opposing tribes at Versailles, pulled between the parties of Étienne François, duc de Choiseul (1719-1785), Chief Minister of the King, Mesdames Tantes, the daughters of Louis XV, and the king's mistress, Madame du Barry (1743-1793). She kept up an extensive correspondence with her mother, who offered her much advice about daily life and periodically urged her to ensure she was on the right side of the king's mistress.

A QUEEN OF FRANCE (1774-1789)

On 10 May 1774, King Louis XV died. Marie-Antoinette became queen of France and Navarre. However, no heir had been born yet: her intimate relationship with Louis XVI was difficult because the king kept putting off the consummation of the marriage, which did not take place until seven years after the wedding. Obscene pamphlets circulated widely, claiming that the queen had all sorts of relationships with lovers or mistresses.

Her life at court was marked by apathy and profound boredom, which she attempted to overcome by distracting herself: she divided her time between games, the theatre, the opera, masked balls, stays in royal castles, and outfits, each one more lavish than the last. She also surrounded herself with devoted favourites, such as Marie-Louise, princesse de Lamballe (1749-1792), and sought a degree of intimacy, preferring small evening meals at the Petit Trianon to official dinners. She also established a little model village, the Hameau de la Reine, on the edge of the park of the Palace of Versailles, where she found the charms of the countryside. Her search for a simpler life attracted increasing hostility at the conservative court.

The Hameau de la Reine.

Her public image was further tarnished by the Affair of the Diamond Necklace, although in this case she was the victim of brazen scheming by unscrupulous individuals. She was increasingly mocked in popular songs, and experienced a degree of unpopularity within the monarchy.

A WOMAN IN TROUBLE (1789-1793)

Starting with the meeting of the Estates-General in May 1789, she became the target of growing popular discontent. During the uprisings on 5 and 6 October, she was taken by force from Versailles to the Tuileries Palace in Paris, where she then had to stay with the royal family. Opposed to the new Constitutional Monarchy, she appealed for help from her brother Joseph II, now Holy Roman Emperor, and then his successor, her other brother Leopold II (1747-1792). As the situation showed no signs of improving, on 20 June 1791 she fled Paris with her family to join the regiments which had remained faithful to the monarchy, led by Monsieur de Bouillé (1739-1800), but she was stopped two days later in Varennes. This attempt to flee and France's declaration of war on Austria on 3 August 1792 led to riots on 10 August. On that day, the Tuileries Palace was stormed and the royal family sought refuge at the Legislative Assembly, before being incarcerated in the Temple, which became a prison. After the Convention voted for the death of the king, who was executed on 21 January 1793, the queen was imprisoned in the Conciergerie and accused in turn.

Her trial, which began on 13 October 1793, quickly delivered the death sentence. She was guillotined on the morning of 16 October in the Place de la Révolution, now Place de la Concorde, while popular anger desperately attempted to take away her dignity, which she would maintain until the very end. Her remains were placed in an unmarked grave designed to give her an undignified ending, as had been done on 21 January 1793 for her husband. It was not until

1815 and the restoration of the monarchy in France that the royal couple was buried in the Basilica of Saint Denis.

Louis XVIII (1755-1824) built an expiatory chapel (*Chapelle expiatoire*) on the site of the Madeleine Cemetery, where Louis XVI and Marie-Antoinette were initially buried, between 1815 and 1826. The chapel is in the current Square Louis XVI. This is the only place bearing the name of the last Ancien Régime monarch in Paris.

CONTEXT

FRANCE AND AUSTRIA IN THE SECOND HALF OF THE 18TH CENTURY

Enemy powers

In the 18th century, relations between France and Austria were particularly difficult. When Charles VI, Holy Roman Emperor (1685-1740) died, and in accordance with the Pragmatic Sanction of 1713, the Habsburg hereditary possessions went to his eldest daughter, Maria Theresa. A war of succession ensued: Charles VII, the prince-elector of Bavaria (1697-1745), put forward a claim to the throne against her and was a serious pretender. England and the Dutch Republic backed Maria Theresa, whereas Prussia under Frederick II (1712-1786), who wanted to take over Silesia, and the France of Louis XV supported the prince-elector of Bavaria.

France went to war against Austria on land and against England at sea. In 1748, it emerged from the conflict with no gains and greatly weakened. Even worse, it was betrayed by its Prussian ally, which signed a separate peace and managed to recover its territories. When Maria Theresa acceded to the imperial throne, her husband also became emperor. However, he had no power; this remained in the hands of his wife.

Reconciliation in war

Soon, everyone was infuriated by King Frederick II, who embodied the growing power of Prussia. Austria, which had unwillingly been forced to give him the rich province of Silesia, wanted to recover it. Meanwhile, tensions between France and England, linked to their North American possessions, were running high. When Prussia offered its support to England, an incredible reversal of alliances ensued: France and Austria now shared common interests. The resulting conflict, the Seven Years' War (1756-1763), in which France and Austria fought side by side against mainly Prussia and England, was the most important conflict of the 18th century.

At the end of the war, the Treaty of Paris (10 February 1763) established England as a colonial power and Prussia as a military power. France and Austria both emerged weakened. The former had lost its North American colonies and exhausted its troops, while the latter had definitively lost Silesia. The two powers needed each other now more than ever.

Strengthening the Franco-Austrian alliance

Maria Theresa, who was now empress alongside her eldest son, Joseph II, Holy Roman Emperor, ensured the future of her children by securing positions for them which served her dual diplomatic aim: strengthening the alliance with France and standing in the way of Prussia. Through her daughters' marriages, she increased the number of alliances binding Austria to France: her daughter Maria Christina (1742-1798) married one of the sons of the king of Poland, Albert Casimir, Duke of Teschen (1738-1822), who was both a neighbour of Prussia and brother of the dauphine of France; Maria Amalia (1746-1804) married Ferdinand, Duke of Parma (1751-1802), the grandson of Louis XV on his mother's side; and Maria Carolina (1752-1814) married Ferdinand IV of Naples (1751-1814), a Bourbon on his father's side and cousin of the future King Louis XVI on his mother's side.

Unfortunately, Louis, Dauphin of France (1729-1765), died, followed two years later by the dauphine Maria Josepha of Saxony (1731-1767). Once again, Maria Theresa needed to strengthen the French alliance by joining with the new dauphin, Louis-Auguste. She then offered him her daughter Marie-Antoinette's hand in marriage, a particularly attractive union because it ensured that one of her daughters would become queen of France.

THE COURT

The comfort of Vienna

In Vienna, Marie-Antoinette was brought up in a simple

court, where the imperial children were educated far from the crowd. The intimacy of the family setting was preserved thanks to rooms reserved for the emperor, the empress and their 16 children. The protocol adopted by the House of Habsburg in 1548 had been preserved and was strictly observed at the Spanish court. However, Francis and Maria Theresa found it boring and intended to raise their children close to them. The children's governesses thus had to regularly report on their smallest actions and movement to the empress. However, the youngest children received less supervision.

Countess von Brandeis, who was in charges of the youngest children, quickly succumbed to Marie-Antoinette's charms. She forgave her all her whims and even did her homework for her. Consequently, she was soon replaced by Countess Lerchenfeld, who was considered to be stricter. This change proved necessary: at the age of ten, Marie-Antoinette still struggled to read and write German, her native language. She also had difficulty learning the basics of foreign languages such as French and Italian, which her brothers and sisters spoke fluently.

Did you know?

On 13 October 1762, a young prodigy was presented at the Viennese Court, accompanied by his father. The child, who had just turned six, played the harpsichord beautifully. He gave a recital for the imperial family in the Hall of Mirrors at the Schönbrunn Palace. At the end of the recital, he mischievously leapt onto the knees of the empress, who kissed him. He then slipped on the floor and was caught by the young Marie-Antoinette, who was two months older than him. To thank her, the little boy asked her if she would agree to marry him. We do not know what the young archduchess answered, but the boy returned happily to his father's arms. This young boy was none other than Wolfgang Amadeus Mozart (1756-1791).

The strictness of Versailles

The court of Versailles, which the young dauphine entered a few years later, was very different to the court she was used to. Etiquette there was a subtle art, and had been further strengthened by Louis XIV a few decades earlier. The smallest faux pas became a scandal, which would make or break reputations. As such, on Marie-Antoinette's wedding night, the Princesses of Lorraine, relatives of the new dauphine, were authorised to dance with the duchesses, which horrified the nobility. Conversely, the court hypocritically tolerated the official royal mistress, who lived a life fit for a queen.

From her arrival, Marie-Antoinette felt ill at ease in this stuffy environment. She was manipulated by the main clans vying for power and influence: Mesdames Tantes, the daughters of Louis XV, Marie Adélaïde (1732-1800), Victoire (1733-1799) and Sophie (1734-1782), strict spinsters, supported her. They taught her to mistrust, and even hate, the king's mistress, whom Marie-Antoinette refused to speak to for a long time. Forced by her mother and the Austrian ambassador, Florimond Claude, comte de Mercy-Argenteau (1727-1794), on 1 January 1772, she said to her simply "There are a lot of people at Versailles today". The ice was broken, but the dauphine felt humiliated and gradually distanced herself from Mesdames Tantes.

When she became queen, she did not try to change etiquette, preferring instead to avoid it. As soon as she could, she left the formality of Versailles to live a more intimate life at the Petit Trianon. This pavilion, built by Louis XV for his mistress Madame de Pompadour (1721-1764), was given to her by Louis XVI. She spent afternoons there, and dined with her favourites and the guests of the moment without worrying about protocol. Due to a lack of space, everyone went back to Versailles to sleep, apart from the queen and a small number of privileged others. At the Hameau she had had built for herself, Marie-Antoinette dressed simply, away from the pomp of court.

SIGNIFICANT MOMENTS

PORTRAIT

Marie-Antoinette had a good figure and was quite pretty, but had a slightly protruding jaw, which her official portraitist Madame Lebrun (1755-1842) would always try to erase.

Portrait of Marie-Antoinette painted by Madame Lebrun.

When her intimate relationship with Louis XVI proved difficult, the couple received much advice, including from Marie-Antoinette's brother Joseph. He even came to Versailles with this very aim. It was an important issue, because the future of the dynasty needed to be ensured. However, rumours took precedence over facts to the sole discredit of the queen, who was accused of having many lovers. Although it is possible that she had a relationship with the Swedish count Hans Axel von Fersen (1755-1810), at present there is no way of confirming this.

Marie-Antoinette had a very pronounced character. Everything bored her and she had to be constantly entertained with balls, plays or games. She was also capricious and demanded that her desires be satisfied immediately: under her orders, a particular apartment had to be redecorated as quickly as possible, or a new dress had to be brought to her as soon as it was made, no matter the cost. In this, she did not differ from other princesses, queens and even royal mistresses of the time, who had much more extravagant and costly whims than she did. Indeed, although she was criticised for her financial profligacy (she was later nicknamed *Madame Déficit*), we now know that the sums spent were part of ordinary life at court, and that this court's expenses were the same as or lower than those of previous reigns.

Music and the theatre were her favoured modes of entertainment. She set up a small theatre at the Trianon, where in particular plays by Beaumarchais (French writer, 1732-1799), including *The Barber of Seville*, were performed. She sometimes played a variety of roles, which amused her friends and Louis XVI. She invited the German composer Christoph Willibald Gluck (1714-1787), her former music teacher from Vienna, to the court, and also encouraged the French composer André Grétry (1741-1813), who she promoted as director of her personal music.

THE AFFAIR OF THE DIAMOND NECKLACE

The Affair of the Diamond Necklace resulted from an immense swindle organised by Jeanne de Valois-Saint-Rémy, comtesse de la Motte (1756-1791), her husband and one of their friends, Armand Gabriel Rétaux de Villette (1759-1797), a notorious forger. Their two victims were the Cardinal de Rohan (1734-1803), bishop of Strasbourg, and Marie-Antoinette, whose name would be wrongly tarnished as a result of the affair.

Some years earlier, the jewellers had made a necklace with sumptuous diamonds. They tried to sell it at court, but Marie-Antoinette refused.

The diamond necklace.

The Comtesse de la Motte, who had become the mistress of the naïve Cardinal de Rohan, who was at that time out of favour, convinced him to buy the necklace on credit for Marie-Antoinette.

On 28 December 1784, the Comtesse de la Motte made the jewellers believe that the 2840-carat necklace, which was worth 1.6 million livres (around 13 million pounds), would be bought by the queen using the Cardinal de Rohan as an intermediary. The cardinal trusted her and complied with the plan, thinking that this would win him back the favour of the queen. Meanwhile, the Comtesse de la Motte took possession of the necklace, which was immediately stripped of its jewels so that they could be resold in Paris, Brussels and London.

The jewellers and the Cardinal de Rohan were surprised that the queen was not wearing the necklace, as it was the most extraordinary piece of jewellery ever made. The jeweller Boehmer was worried about future payments and went to Versailles. The queen was dumbfounded to learn of the affair, and Louis XVI was informed of the swindle on 14 August 1785. The Cardinal de Rohan was immediately arrested in the middle of the Hall of Mirrors, in front of the entire court. It was an enormous scandal.

A public trial began before the *parlement* of Paris in May 1786. The cardinal was acquitted, while the Comtesse de la Motte was sentenced to life imprisonment and her husband to the galleys. However, Marie-Antoinette was deeply humiliated. The publicity of the affair discredited the queen: public opinion played its part and some continued to believe that the she was involved in the scheme. Insulting pamphlets circulated. The breakdown of trust between the people and Marie-Antoinette was now underway.

THE FLIGHT TO VARENNES

After the revolutionary days of October 1789, the royal family was practically under house arrest at the Tuileries Palace in Paris. Each member of the family was placed under the protection, but also the surveillance, of the Marquis de Lafayette (1757-1834), commander-in-chief of the National Guard. From that point, those close to them had the idea of sheltering them outside Paris, but it was not until September 1790 that the Bishop of Pamiers suggested going away. The plan was simple: they would travel to the stronghold of Montmédy, where the Marquis de Bouillé would have raised an army, ready to lend its support to the sovereigns. In a six-person coach drawn by six horses, the royal family would travel under false identities. The idea was to make everyone believe that the convoy comprised a baroness who was the widow of a Russian officer and her children, travelling to Frankfurt. The baroness would be played by the governess of the royal children, the children by the dauphin and his sister, the governess of the children by Marie-Antoinette, the valet of the baroness by Louis XVI, and her female companion by Élisabeth of France, the king's sister (1764-1794).

During the night of the 20 to 21 June, helped by von Fersen, the royal family left the Tuileries Palace and came out onto the Rue de l'Échelle, near the Louvre. They then left Paris without a hitch. At 7am, the king's manservant raised the alarm, and Lafayette spread the news that there had been a kidnapping, while dispatching troops in all directions to capture them. The coach had already passed Châlons by the end of the afternoon.

At 11pm, the coach, which has reached Varennes, was stopped on the order of the Assembly. Marie-Antoinette spent the night there before being brought back to Paris under heavy guard. After a three-day journey with stops in Châlons and Meaux, the royal family passed through Paris in the afternoon of 25 June, amid a silent crowd. At 10pm, the rage of the masses exploded when the procession reached the Tuileries.

In spite of the political testament left by Louis XVI before his departure, in which he accepted, or pretended to accept, a constitutional monarchy, everyone saw the flight as the king abandoning his people and rallying foreign forces against France; in other words, as an act of high treason. This was a turning point in the Revolution, with considerable consequences: supporters of the abolition of the monarchy, who had until then been in the minority, took the upper hand, and Marie-Antoinette was accused of colluding with the enemy; from then onwards, she was referred to as "the Austrian woman" or "the monster".

MARIE ANTOINETTE SYNDROME

According to legend, the day after Varennes – and not, as is widely claimed, the day before her execution – Marie-Antoinette's hair turned completely white. This phenomenon is now known as Marie Antoinette syndrome. However, there are reported cases of it well before that. The English philosopher and politician Thomas More (1478-1535) allegedly suffered from it the day before his execution. This syndrome, which results from extreme stress or a severe psychological shock, is still under debate within the scientific community, but has given rise to the French expression "se faire des cheveux blancs" ("to give oneself white hair"), meaning "to worry oneself sick".

Marie Antoinette in the Temple Prison, painting by Alexander Kucharsky, 1793.

THE TRIAL OF THE WIDOW CAPET

More than six months after the execution of Louis XVI, the queen was imprisoned in the Conciergerie on 2 August 1793. She had been separated from her children and the king's sister for several weeks and was now alone. She was also reportedly suffering from cancer, which was speeding up her death. For the revolutionaries who were in power, as the monarchy had been abolished and the king had been executed, Marie-Antoinette was now of no political interest. She therefore had to be eliminated as soon as possible.

Her trial began on 13 October 1793 before the Revolutionary Tribunal, presided by Martial Joseph Armand Herman (1749-1795). The public prosecutor was the fearsome Antoine Quentin Fouquier-Tinville (1746-1795), known for his harshness, arbitrariness and extreme violence towards the Ancien Régime. Marie-Antoinette was therefore choice prey for him. The accusation was drawn up in all haste. It lacked evidence and had fairly little content. Consequently, the defendant was charged with every accusation possible.

Queen Marie-Antoinette before the Revolutionary Tribunal.

Marie-Antoinette, the widow of Louis Capet, was first accused of high treason. She had allegedly colluded with foreign powers against France. She was then accused of being the main instigator of her husband's treason. Finally, she was blamed for everything bad in France over the previous years and declared a sworn enemy of the French nation. The witnesses presented were all for the prosecution. However, the worst was yet to come: the ferocious Jacques-René Hébert (politician, 1757-1794), who had just become leader of the *sans-culottes* (the revolutionaries) decided to make the dauphin testify against his mother. Marie-Antoinette was then accused of incest. Shocked and outraged, at first she did not respond. Faced with an astonished jury, she eventually replied: "I appeal to the conscience and feelings of every mother present, to declare if there by one amongst you who does not shudder at the idea of such horrors" (cited in Gelardi, 2009). The entire crowd, and particularly the women, applauded.

The jury eventually found her guilty of intelligence with the enemy and conspiracy against the Republic. She was sentenced to death without the possibility of appeal on 16 October 1793, and taken in a cart – whereas Louis XVI had been driven in a carriage – shortly after midday on the same day to the Place de la Révolution to be guillotined.

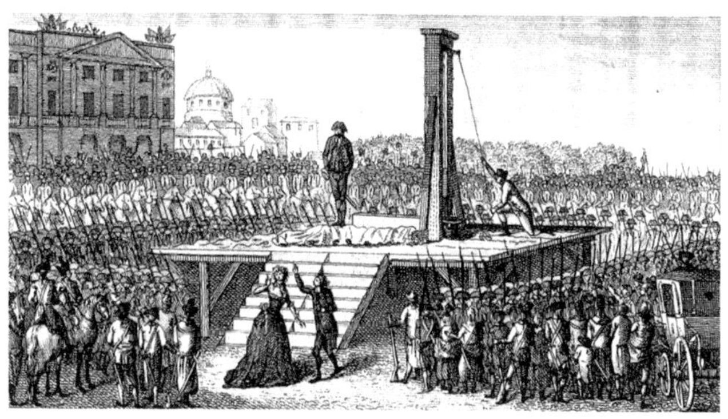

Execution of Marie-Antoinette, 1793.

IMPACT

MARIE-ANTOINETTE'S DESCENDANTS

Marie-Antoinette had four children. They are depicted by an empty cradle in Madame Lebrun's famous 1787 painting *Marie Antoinette and her children*.

Marie Antoinette and her children, painting by Madame Lebrun, 1787.

Her eldest daughter, Marie-Thérèse Charlotte (1778-1851), was a miracle child, after a marriage that went unconsummated for a long time. Better known as Madame Royale, she would be the only one to survive the French Revolution. She remained imprisoned in the Temple after the death of her mother, and was released on 19 December 1795. She was then handed over to the Austrian envoys in Basel, in exchange for a number of French political prisoners held in Austria. In 1799, she married her cousin Louis-Antoine, duc d'Angoulême (1775-1844), the son of the future Charles X of France (1757-1836). A symbol of the Restoration from 1814, she was very briefly queen of France, on 2 August 1830, before Louis Philippe I (1773-1850) took power. As she had no children, she yielded the throne to her nephew Henry, comte de Chambord (1820-1883), and would play a prominent role in the Legitimist movement until her death in Austria in 1851.

Marie-Antoinette's second child, Louis Joseph, was the eagerly awaited dauphin, their heir to the Bourbon throne. He was intelligent but his health was fragile, and he died of tuberculosis on 4 June 1789, at the age of eight, during the meeting of the Estates-General. Neither Marie-Antoinette nor the king had the time to mourn their little boy.

Louis-Charles (1785-1795), the couple's third child, became dauphin when his brother died in 1789. He was imprisoned with his parents following the storming of the Tuileries on 10 August 1792, and was educated by his father until the latter was executed in January 1793. The child, who took the name of Louis XVII, was the Royalist's great hope. He then lived with Marie-Antoinette until 3 July 1793. He was subsequently taken away from his mother on the orders of the Committee of Public Safety, he was put in the care of the cobbler Antoine Simon (1736-1794) and his wife until January 1794. He was then abandoned in very precarious circumstances for six months. Suffering from tuberculosis, he died in prison on 8 June 1795. Rumours of kidnapping or substitution quickly emerged, but it seems today that these were unfounded.

The last child of Marie-Antoinette and Louis XVI, Sophie Hélène Beatrix, died at the age of 11 months at Versailles. She was buried at the Royal Basilica of Saint Denis. Her death left the royal couple very shaken.

A BREAK BETWEEN THE MONARCHY AND THE FRENCH PEOPLE

The role played by Marie-Antoinette in political life until 1789, first as dauphine and then as queen of France, is quite modest, and her interventions were not at all calculated. Unlike her mother, Maria Theresa, she was not a woman of politics, and preferred to think about frivolous topics. Conversely, from 1789 onwards, she certainly tried to influence events to hold back change, with a far less flexible stance than Louis XVI, harbouring the secret hope that everything would go back to how it was before. As such, she was one of the elements that would lead to the breakdown of trust between the monarchy and the French people in the late 18th century.

However, Marie-Antoinette's real blunders and extravagances were greatly magnified by her errors of communication. Beyond that, the development of the press and its use of events after the fact to blow inconsequential incidents out of all proportion played a major role in the manipulation of public opinion. The Affair of the Diamond Necklace illustrates this perfectly. Instead of being hushed up, the affair spread with the public arrest of the Cardinal de Rohan in front of the entire court and then his trial at the *parlement*, in full view of the public. This severely tarnished the queen's reputation, even though she was completely innocent. Another example is her desire to lead a simpler life at the Hameau de la Reine. Instead of working in her favour, as something that brought her closer to her people, Marie-Antoinette's choice was quickly seen as a costly flight of fancy.

Likewise, the press retrospectively depicted the Lisbon earthquake on 1 November 1755 (the day before Marie-Antoinette was born) and the people killed by fireworks set off in Paris on 30 May 1770 as part of the celebrations of Marie-Antoinette and Louis XVI's wedding as early warning signs indicating coming catastrophes.

In fact, her correspondence with the Comte de Mercy-Argenteau provides undeniable proof of her wish to return to a strong monarchy as soon as possible. Conversely, the accusation that she wanted to brutally repress the popular movements in Paris in April 1792 is a false story peddled by her opponents.

MYTH AND CONTROVERSY

On her death, a double myth was created. On the one hand, the revolutionaries of the time, then the republicans of the 19th century, based on the queen's various blunders and her stances during the Revolution, depicted her as a bloodthirsty Fury, the damned soul of the Counter-Revolution. This sentiment was intensified by the newspapers, which disseminated the idea. This phenomenon spread further during the Third Republic, once the monarchy had been definitively abolished in France.

On the other hand, a counter-myth emerged at the same time. Ardent defenders of the monarchy, both in France and abroad, considered her as a humiliated sovereign who needed to be protected against bloodthirsty revolutionaries. They stressed the queen's dignity during her trial and execution in order to turn her into a martyr. The Restoration in 1815 did not hesitate to take up this thread until 1830. Even today, her followers leave flowers at the Expiatory Chapel in Paris or in the gardens of Versailles on 16 October, the anniversary of her death.

Finally, a fairly small minority of historians consider her to be scatterbrained, inconsistent, clumsy and frivolous, dragged in spite of herself into events that she did not understand.

The truth is undoubtedly somewhere between all these interpretations.

SUMMARY

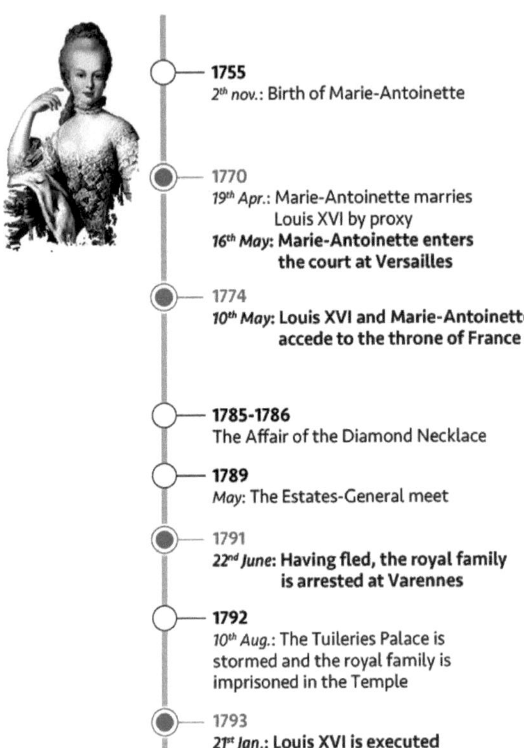

1755
2th nov.: Birth of Marie-Antoinette

1770
19th Apr.: Marie-Antoinette marries
    Louis XVI by proxy
**16th May: Marie-Antoinette enters
    the court at Versailles**

1774
**10th May: Louis XVI and Marie-Antoinette
    accede to the throne of France**

1785-1786
The Affair of the Diamond Necklace

1789
May: The Estates-General meet

1791
**22nd June: Having fled, the royal family
    is arrested at Varennes**

1792
10th Aug.: The Tuileries Palace is
stormed and the royal family is
imprisoned in the Temple

1793
21st Jan.: Louis XVI is executed
13rd Oct.: Marie-Antoinette's trial begins
**16th Oct.: Marie-Antoinette is sentenced
    and executed**

1815
Louis XVI and Marie-Antoinette are
buried in the Basilica of Saint Denis

- Marie-Antoinette, Archduchess of Austria, was one of the daughters of Francis I, Holy Roman Emperor, and his wife, the Empress Maria Theresa. With the aim of strengthening the alliance between the Habsburgs and the Bourbons, her mother arranged a marriage with Louis-Auguste, the grandson and heir of King Louis XV of France. Marie-Antoinette married the dauphin in April-May 1770, and was thus destined to become queen of France.

- The young dauphine then went to Versailles at age of 14. For four years, the cheerful young woman was at the centre of a small circle while trying to find her place amid the rival clans which, between the daughters of Louis XV and his mistress Madame du Barry, stirred up scandal and intrigues at court.

- After becoming queen of France and Navarre on 10 May 1774, she staved off boredom with frivolous entertainment, a mixture of games, theatre and interior decoration, particularly at the Petit Trianon and at the Hameau de la Reine, a model farm that she had built from scratch.

- She was remote from the people and made an increasing number of blunders, for example in the Affair of the Diamond Necklace, which tarnished her reputation.

- Caught up in the revolutionary upheaval, Marie-Antoinette struggled to influence the course of events, and became increasingly unpopular. After her attempt to flee with the rest of the royal family and their arrest in Varennes on 21 June 1791, the revolutionary press systematically targeted her.

- After the Tuileries Palace was stormed on 10 August 1792, she was imprisoned in the Temple, then, after the execution of Louis XVI, in the Conciergerie, where she would remain until her trial. She was sentenced to death and guillotined, at the age of 37, on 16 October 1793 in the Place de la Révolution in Paris.

- Today, Marie-Antoinette is surrounded by myths and controversy, with depictions of her ranging from a martyr to the Revolution to a criminal despot. Whatever the truth may be, this key figure of French history always provokes strong opinions.

We want to hear from you!
Leave a comment on your online library
and share your favourite books on social media!

FIND OUT MORE

BIBLIOGRAPHY

- Bertière, S. (2002) *Marie-Antoinette l'insoumise*. Paris: Éditions de Fallois.
- De Decker, M. (2005) *Marie-Antoinette : les dangereuses liaisons de la reine*. Paris: Belfond.
- Fauveau, J.-C. (2007) *Le prince Louis cardinal de Rohan-Guéméné ou les diamants du roi*. Paris: L'Harmattan.
- Gelardi, J.P. (2009) *In Triumph's Wake: Royal Mothers, Tragic Daughters and the Price They Paid for Glory*. New York: St. Martin's Press.
- Lever, E. (2006) *Marie Antoinette: The Last Queen of France*. London: Piatkus Books.

ADDITIONAL SOURCES

- Bashor, W. (2016) *Marie Antoinette's Darkest Days: Prisoner No. 280 in the Conciergerie*. Lanham, Maryland: Rowman & Littlefield.
- Beckman, J. (2014) *How to Ruin a Queen: Marie Antoinette, the Stolen Diamonds and the Scandal that Shook the French Throne*. London: John Murray.
- Fraser, A. (2002) *Marie Antoinette*. London: Weidenfeld and Nicolson.
- Walton, G. (2016) *Marie Antoinette's Confidante: The Rise and Fall of the Princesse de Lamballe*. Barnsley: Pen and Sword History.
- Zweig, S. (2010) *Marie Antoinette*. Trans. Paul, C. and Paul, E. London: Pushkin Press.

ICONOGRAPHIC SOURCES

- Marie-Antoinette's wedding celebrations in the opera hall at Versailles, 1770. Royalty-free reproduction picture.
- The Hameau de la Reine. Royalty-free reproduction picture.
- Portrait of Marie-Antoinette painted by Madame Lebrun. Royalty-free reproduction picture.
- The Diamond Necklace. Royalty-free reproduction picture.
- *Marie Antoinette in the Temple Prison*, painting by Alexander Kucharsky, 1793. Royalty-free reproduction picture.
- Queen Marie-Antoinette before the Revolutionary Tribunal. Royalty-free reproduction picture.
- Execution of Marie-Antoinette, 1793. Royalty-free reproduction picture.
- *Marie Antoinette and her childr*en, painting by Madame Lebrun, 1787. Royalty-free reproduction picture.

FILMS AND DOCUMENTARIES

- *Si Versailles m'était conté.* (1954) [Film]. Sascha Guitry. Dir. France: Cocinex.
- *Le Chevalier de Maison Rouge.* (1963) [TV miniseries]. Claude Barma. Dir. France: Office de Radiodiffusion Télévision Française, RAI Radiotelevisione Italiana, Société Nouvelle Pathé Cinéma.
- *La Nuit de Varennes.* (1982) [Film]. Ettore Scola. Dir. France: Opera Film Produzione, France 3, Gaumont.

- *La Révolution Française.* (1989) [Film]. Robert Enrico and Richard T. Heffron. Dirs. France: Les Films Ariana, Films A2, Laura Film, Antea Cinematografia, Alcor Films, Alliance Communications Corporation.
- *Marie Antoinette.* (2006) [Film]. Sofia Coppola. Dir. USA/France/Japan: Columbia Pictures Corporation.

www.50minutes.com

Ebook EAN: 9782806290038

Paperback EAN: 9782806293473

Legal Deposit: D/2017/12603/50

Cover: © Primento

Digital conception by Primento, the digital partner of publishers.